IMAGES
of America

FLORIDA'S
SHIPWRECKS

In this dramatic photograph, a crippled tanker, torpedoed by a German U-boat, drifts abandoned off the Florida coast. Marauding U-boats sunk over 40 Allied ships unprepared for war off Florida's shores. (Courtesy of author.)

ON THE COVER: Photographed on August 2, 1899, the cover image captures various disabled ships aground at Dog Island after the 1899 hurricane. From left to right are the American schooner *James A. Garfield* (background), the Norwegian bark *Vale* (foreground), and the Norwegian bark *Jafnhar*. While the *James A. Garfield* was refloated, the *Vale* and *Jafnhar* were abandoned, and their remains still rest in the shallow water of Shipping Cove on the west end of Dog Island. (Courtesy of Florida State Archives.)

IMAGES
of America

FLORIDA'S
SHIPWRECKS

Michael Barnette

ARCADIA
PUBLISHING

Published by Arcadia Publishing
Charleston, South Carolina

Printed in the United States of America

Library of Congress Catalog Card Number: 2008921895

For all general information contact Arcadia Publishing at:
Telephone 843-853-2070
Fax 843-853-0044
E-mail sales@arcadiapublishing.com
For customer service and orders:
Toll-Free 1-888-313-2665

Visit us on the Internet at www.arcadiapublishing.com

This view shows the screw on the wreck of an unidentified steamer, possibly the *Alicia A. Washburn*, off Carrabelle. The small screw steamer *Washburn* was built by Ward, Stanton, and Company in Newburg, New York, in 1880. She was 125 feet in length, 30 feet in breadth, and displaced 210 tons. On January 9, 1886, en route from Mobile, Alabama, to New York, she caught fire and was abandoned to sink 25 miles off St. George Island. (Courtesy of author.)

CONTENTS

ACKNOWLEDGMENTS

I would first like to thank my parents, Jerry and Jill Barnette, who offered constant support in my pursuits while I was growing up. After I showed an interest in marine biology at an early age, they helped fuel my curiosity and passion for the ocean. Without their support, it is doubtful I would have followed the same path in life.

Since moving to Florida in 1999, I have had the pleasure of meeting numerous individuals who have assisted with my efforts to research and document local shipwrecks. Most notably, I would like to acknowledge my fellow divers of the Association of Underwater Explorers, who have traveled with me to dive Florida shipwrecks near and far. I would like to particularly thank Joe Citelli for his consistent friendship and support over the years. Other individuals who have helped with this project include Fernando José García Echegoyen; the venerable Robert "Frogfoot" Weller; N. Adam Watson of the Florida State Archives; the entire crew at Halcyon; and my editor, Luke Cunningham.

Finally, this project would not have been possible without the enduring encouragement and support of my wife, Melanie. She has been extremely understanding of my sometimes insane pursuit of history. Thanks, baby.

INTRODUCTION

It is no secret that shipwrecks have the ability to capture the imagination. Whether it is the vessels' fascinating service histories, the drama of the actual sinking events, or the exploration of their submerged remains, shipwrecks are compelling. Since the early exploration of the Florida peninsula in the 16th century, shipwrecks have become an integral part of the state's maritime history.

"After the Storm" begins by revealing a few events related to one of the principal shipwreck instruments—hurricanes. Hurricanes are a fact of life in Florida, but while Florida residents have grown accustomed to their annual inconvenience, hurricanes were a constant menace to shipping. Their influence will lead the reader into the next section, "River of Gold," a reference to the massive amounts of treasure streaming along the coast toward Spain. No work on Florida shipwrecks would be complete without an overview of these treasure fleets. The wreck of the *Atocha* and its subsequent rediscovery by Mel Fisher is perhaps one of the most-publicized episodes in Florida shipwreck history. On a somewhat more idyllic journey, "Coursing Waters" will carry the reader through a portion of the state's maritime history often forgotten. Before rail was laid and roads were paved, riverine and coastal commerce were integral parts of Florida's development. On a more somber note, "Legacy of War" documents the numerous war casualties that occurred off Florida's shores. Florida was totally unprepared for the arrival of German U-boats in early 1942. That lack of preparation allowed the undersea marauders to sink close to 40 vessels in fairly short order. Today the rusting hulks of numerous tankers and freighters sent to the bottom by the German Kriegsmarine serve as mute testimony to the far-reaching effects of World War II. Lastly, "That Sinking Feeling" illustrates several other Florida wreck events, some of which are recent. Even with advances in technology, such as accurate weather forecasting, satellite navigation, and radar, additional vessels still plunge to the bottom every year. If nothing else, the final chapter is a stark reminder that the sea is an unforgiving host.

The photographs within this book appear courtesy of numerous archives and private collections, and those without credits were taken from my personal collection, compiled from years of research and dive expeditions. This book is an attempt to share a small cross-section of Florida shipwreck history. It is hoped that within these pages, readers will be both entertained and educated.

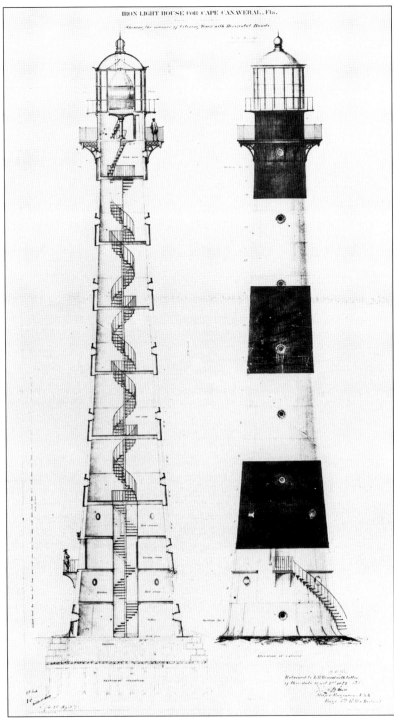

Cape Canaveral Light is documented in engineering drawings drafted in April 1873. Canaveral Light, as well as the other lighthouses constructed in the late 19th and early 20th centuries, helped to ward off vessels from straying too close to dangerous portions of the coast. (Courtesy of Mark Mondano Collection.)

One

AFTER THE STORM

Pictured are the remains of the American schooner *Nathan F. Cobb*, wrecked on Ormond Beach. She was sailing for New York with a cargo of lumber when a storm stripped away her masts and cast the disabled vessel onto the beach in December 1896. The *Nathan F. Cobb* was built in November 1890 in Bath, Maine, and was 167.2 feet long, 35.1 feet on the beam, and displaced 674 tons. (Courtesy of Florida State Archives.)

The *City of Vera Cruz* was a wooden-hulled, brigantine-rigged steamship built in 1874 on Long Island, New York, by the John English shipyard. Built for Alexandre and Sons for the New York–to-Havana route, the passenger/freighter was 296 feet long with a 37-foot beam and a 26-foot draft. Departing from New York on August 25, 1880, the *City of Vera Cruz* headed to Havana carrying 28 passengers, 49 crew members, and a wide variety of freight. On August 28, the steamer encountered a massive hurricane. Pummeled mercilessly, she eventually sank just north of Cape Canaveral. Miraculously, of the 77 on board, 11 survivors made it safely to the beach after spending over 24 hours in the water. (Courtesy of Mark Mondano Collection.)

At left, a diver swims over one of the boilers on the wreck of the *City of Vera Cruz*. When she was partially salvaged in the 1980s, numerous artifacts were recovered. Today the wreck rests in 80 feet of water, with the engine and boilers rising to within 55 feet of the surface.

Built in 1882 at a Philadelphia, Pennsylvania, shipyard and home ported in Greenport, New York, the wooden-hulled tug *Commodore* (above) was 122 feet long, 21 feet wide, and displaced 178 tons. On December 31, 1896, she departed Jacksonville with 15 tons of arms and ammunition on a filibustering run to Cuba. Filibustering, or the covert transport (smuggling) of guns, munitions, and supplies, had become a popular and profitable exercise in the waning years of the 19th century. En route, the *Commodore* began taking on water in rough seas and eventually capsized off Daytona Beach on January 2, 1897, claiming four lives. (Courtesy of Ponce de Leon Inlet Lighthouse Preservation Association.)

One of the passengers on board the *Commodore* was Stephen Crane, author of *The Red Badge of Courage*. Crane joined the crew intending to cover the war in Cuba. Instead he was presented with another story of struggle during the sinking of the tug, which he later vividly captured in the short story "The Open Boat: A Tale Intended to be After the Fact. Being the Experience of Four Men Sunk from the Steamer *Commodore*." Originally published in *Scribner's Magazine* in June 1897, "The Open Boat" is based on the real-life events that followed the sinking of the *Commodore*, as Crane and three other survivors drifted in a 10-foot dinghy for over 24 hours. He is pictured here with his wife, Cora, in 1899. (Courtesy of Florida State Archives.)

Photographed on August 2, 1899, the above image documents numerous ships wrecked at Dog Island on the Florida Panhandle. Pictured from left to right are the Norwegian bark *Jafnhar*; the American schooner *James A. Garfield* (in foreground); the American schooner *Mary E. Morse* (in background); the Russian bark *Latava* (dismasted, beyond the *Morse*); the American barkentine *Vivette*; and an unidentified wreck beyond the tugboat. The Norwegian bark *Vale* and an unidentified wreck can be seen in the distance. Of the nine vessels wrecked at Dog Island during the August 1899 hurricane, four were not refloated and were eventually abandoned: the *Jafnhar*, *Vale*, *Latava*, and *Cortesia*. (Courtesy of Florida State Archives.)

The image above demonstrates the power of the August 1899 hurricane, with the masts of this ship snapped like twigs and the remainder of the deck in ruins. Based on the angle of this picture, it may be a view of the Russian bark *Latava*, which was wrecked at Dog Island. (Courtesy of Florida State Archives.)

Another victim of the August 1899 hurricane, the Norwegian bark *Hindoo* (pictured above) was blown ashore at St. George Island. The *Hindoo*, built in July 1877 at Apenrade, Germany, was 147.1 feet long, 31.5 feet wide, and displaced 554 tons. She was successfully refloated and repaired, and eventually reentered service as a barge. (Courtesy of Florida State Archives.)

The middle of a forest is definitely not the place you would expect to find a large sailing ship, but that is just where the August 1899 hurricane delivered this vessel. The 168-foot-long schooner *Warren Adams*, built in July 1884 at Bowdoinham, Maine, was carried into the woods on St. George Island during the storm. Due to damage sustained from the grounding, the *Warren Adams* was condemned in September 1899. (Courtesy of Florida State Archives.)

This picture captures the debris-strewn beach immediately south of Gilbert's Bar House of Refuge on Hutchinson Island near Stuart following a storm in 1904. The lumber was cargo from the Italian bark *Georges Valentine*, which wrecked directly offshore of the U.S. Lifesaving Service outpost during the October 16th storm. Originally built as the bark *Cape Clear* by Bowdler, Chaffer, and Company at Liverpool in March 1869, the *Georges Valentine* was 189.7 feet in length, 31.2 feet in breadth, and displaced 882 tons. (Courtesy of Florida State Archives.)

Curious onlookers inspect the shattered hulk of the *Georges Valentine* in this 1904 image. Also sunk in the same storm as the *Valentine* was the 200-foot-long sailing ship *Cosme Calzada*, which came to grief just north of Gilbert's Bar House of Refuge. The 1,405-ton *Calzada* was built in 1869 by Curtis Smith and Company of Boston, Massachusetts. Aside from one man who became entangled in rigging and drowned, the entire crew made it to the beach safely and eventually joined the survivors of the *Georges Valentine* at the house of refuge. It was not uncommon for beaches to be strewn for miles with debris and bodies in the wake of a major storm. (Courtesy of Florida State Archives.)

On September 27, 1906, a hurricane slammed into Pensacola, devastating the local shipping industry. Known as the "Great Hurricane," the storm struck the city in the early hours of the morning. In this picture, a grounded schooner rests amidst a sea of lumber. (Courtesy of Florida State Archives.)

Here the yawl *Clara R. Grimes* is seen aground at the lumber wharf in Pensacola Harbor after the September 1906 hurricane. Lumber has been an important industry in the Florida Panhandle, especially in Pensacola, where it has been exported since 1743. (Courtesy of Florida State Archives.)

Destruction around Pensacola Harbor from the September 1906 hurricane included the steamers *Monarch* and *Mary Lee*, surrounded by lumber, debris, and swamped lifeboats. (Courtesy of Florida State Archives.)

Few ships in Pensacola Harbor escaped unscathed from the 1906 hurricane. In this picture, the two unidentified ships at right are aground and damaged. Of special note is the vessel with damaged rigging at left, the *Avanti*. The *Avanti* was originally built as the *Killean* by John Reid and Company of Port Glasgow, Scotland, for Mackinnon, Frew, and Company of Liverpool in January 1875. The two-decked, three-masted, iron-hulled vessel was 261.4 feet in length, 39.3 feet in breadth, and displaced 1,862 tons. Following repairs, she sailed for Montevideo with a cargo of lumber, only to sink days later on January 22, 1907, in the Dry Tortugas. The wreck of the *Avanti*, better known as the "Windjammer Wreck," is visited by hundreds of divers annually. (Courtesy of Florida State Archives.)

The steel-hulled paddle steamer *St. Lucie* (above) was 122 feet long, 24 feet wide, and displaced 105 tons. Henry Flagler eventually bought the *St. Lucie* in support of the construction of his Overseas Railroad through the Florida Keys. On October 17, 1906, the *St. Lucie* left the Florida East Coast Railway terminal dock in Miami and headed out into Biscayne Bay with a load of machinery. The steamer also carried approximately 120 passengers and crew, pushing a barge carrying fresh water for the workers on Knight's Key. Capt. Steve Bravo commanded the *St. Lucie* as she made her way south on a routine trip. Unbeknownst to Captain Bravo, however, a fierce hurricane was bearing down on his ship. (Courtesy of Florida State Archives.)

The *St. Lucie* was no match for the 120-mile-per-hour winds she encountered, and the steamer was soon swamped and sunk in the shallow water adjacent to Elliot Key. Over 30 bodies washed up on Elliot and Soldier Keys during the following days. While the Lloyd's Register listed 97 people on board and 21 fatalities, the exact number of dead from the *St. Lucie* is unknown, as no precise passenger manifest was kept on that fateful trip. The *St. Lucie* was eventually raised, repaired at Miami, and put back in service to support work for the Overseas Railroad. (Courtesy of Florida State Archives.)

In order to support the numerous workers required to perform the work required for the construction of the Overseas Railroad, floating dormitories were created using barges and houseboats known as quarterboats, as pictured above. As the October 1906 hurricane swept over Long Key, *Quarterboat No. 4* lost her moorings and was carried out to sea. The flat-bottomed vessel was soon torn to pieces by the raging Atlantic, and men clung to portions of wreckage as they drifted far out to sea. Several workers were killed outright in the disaster, and others drowned as the wreckage continued to fall apart. Miraculously, almost 70 survivors were picked up by various ships in the days following the hurricane, many off the Bahamas. It is believed, however, that as many as 100 men perished in the wrecking of *Quarterboat No. 4*. (Courtesy of Florida State Archives.)

The sinking of the passenger steamer *Valbanera*, with the loss of as many as 488 lives, represents one of the worst maritime disasters to occur in Florida waters. The *Valbanera*, named in honor of the Virgin of Valvanera, was built in 1906 by the C. Cornell and Company shipyard in Glasgow, Scotland. She was 400 feet in length, 48 feet in breadth, and displaced 12,500 tons. She was propelled by two alternative-triple-expansion Dunsmuir and Jackson 444-horsepower engines capable of carrying her at a maximum speed of 12 knots. Owned by Pinillos, Izquierdo, and Company, the *Valbanera* could transport almost 1,200 passengers in four classes. Here the steamer is illustrated in a Pinillos Company advertisement.

The *Valbanera* is photographed here at the Port of Cadiz in 1907 or 1908. She departed Spain on what would be her final voyage in August 1919, bound for San Juan, Puerto Rico; Santiago de Cuba and Havana, Cuba; Galveston, Texas; and New Orleans, Louisiana. On board were 1,142 passengers and 88 crew members. She arrived at Santiago de Cuba on September 5 after a brief visit in San Juan. Though most passengers had booked passage to Havana, for some unknown reason, 742 passengers disembarked in Santiago. The *Valbanera* steamed for Havana, but strong wind and heavy seas from an approaching storm prevented her from entering port on the evening of September 8. Signals indicated she was headed further offshore to ride out the storm overnight, but when dawn came, she was nowhere to be found. (Courtesy of Fernando José García Echegoyen.)

It was not until September 19 that the wreck of the *Valbanera* was discovered by the U.S.S. *SC-203* resting five miles east of Rebecca Shoal, 46 miles west of Key West, in an area called the Quicksands. Divers were dispatched to recover bodies, but no trace of passengers or crew was ever found. In 1932, Ernest Hemingway published the short story "After the Storm," which was loosely based on the sinking of the *Valbanera*. (Courtesy of Fernando José García Echegoyen.)

While the *Valbanera* was by far the most tragic loss in the September 1919 hurricane, it was definitely not the only casualty. Another victim of the storm was the freighter *Bayronto*, captured in the above undated image. The *Bayronto* was a 400-foot-long freighter built in 1905 by Armstrong, Whitworth, and Company of Newcastle, England. While carrying a cargo of 7,000 tons of wheat from Galveston, Texas, to Marseille, France, she ran headlong into the brutal hurricane on September 10. Fortunately, while the freighter capsized and sank, the entire crew managed to survive the ordeal. (Courtesy of Trevor Saunders.)

The wreck of the *Bayronto* now rests in approximately 100 feet of water off Boca Grande Pass, lying inverted and crippled with the keel reaching upwards to within 75 feet of the surface. The large bronze screw of the *Bayronto* was salvaged in the 1980s, and as a result of the work, the steamer's rudder now rests on the seabed, as seen in the above picture.

The September 1926 hurricane made landfall in the early morning hours of September 19. After the storm passed, locals emerged to find their city in ruins. In this image, a grounded U.S. Coast Guard cutter rests in Bayfront Park. (Courtesy of Florida State Archives.)

Another view of Bayfront Park following the September 1926 hurricane documents the 56-foot-long schooner *Kessie C. Price* high and dry. The *Price* was built in 1888 at Rock Creek, Maryland, but it is unclear if the damage sustained from the grounding ended her career or if she was repaired and put back into service. (Courtesy of Florida State Archives.)

Pictured above, the 143-foot-long luxury yacht *Nohab* was originally built in 1901 at Kiel, Germany, as the *Lensahn* for the Duke of Oldenburg. The yacht was eventually gifted to Kaiser Wilhelm II of Germany, who hosted numerous world leaders and dignitaries, including the Czar of Russia, King George V of England, and Pres. Theodore Roosevelt. Following World War I, the yacht changed hands several times, eventually coming to Florida in late 1925. (Courtesy of Florida State Archives.)

In addition to grounding numerous ships throughout Miami, the September 1926 hurricane sank several vessels, including the yacht *Nohab*. Prior to the storm, she was anchored in Biscayne Bay with an attending crew. At the height of the storm, the yacht capsized, claiming the lives of five of the seven crew members; she is pictured above following her sinking. The *Nohab* was eventually raised and towed to Tampa to be overhauled. However, the requisite repairs were ultimately deemed cost prohibitive, and the once palatial yacht was towed out of Tampa Bay and scuttled in 65 feet of water in 1934. (Courtesy of Florida State Archives.)

Built in 1887 at the Wilmington, Delaware, shipyard of the Pusey and Jones Company, the twin-screw steamer *Tarpon*, pictured in the undated photograph above, was originally launched as the *Naugatuck*. In 1889, the steamer was sold to Henry B. Plant and moved south to expand the reach of Plant's railroads in Florida. In 1902, she was sold to the newly formed Pensacola, St. Andrews, and Gulf Steamship Company. Beginning in 1903, Capt. Willis Green Barrow helmed the *Tarpon* on weekly runs between the ports of Mobile, Alabama; and Pensacola, Panama City, Apalachicola, and Carrabelle, Florida. The captain often said, "God makes the weather, and I make the trip." (Courtesy of Florida State Archives.)

The *Tarpon* is pictured dockside at Apalachicola in 1898 while operating for Henry B. Plant. The steamer began her last voyage on August 30, 1937, in what was to be just another routine trip along the Florida Panhandle. Upon her departure from Mobile, the steamer was burdened with over 200 tons of general cargo, as well as 31 passengers and crew, which left her sitting low in the water. During the journey, the *Tarpon* began leaking from the pounding of heavy seas, but Captain Barrow refused to alter course or risk arriving late. As a result, the *Tarpon* sank on September 1, 1937, taking 18 lives with her, including that of Captain Barrow. (Courtesy of Florida State Archives.)

An unidentified Cuban fishing smack is pictured cast high on the beach of Marco Island by the October 1941 hurricane. (Courtesy of Florida State Archives.)

En route from Manchester, England, to Baton Rouge, Louisiana, the Greek-owned freighter *Amaryllis* ran aground on September 8, 1965, because of storm-churned seas created by Hurricane Betsy. As depicted in the above image, the 442-foot freighter slowly rusted for almost three years while beached on Singer Island, approximately four miles north of Palm Beach, before her superstructure was razed and she was towed offshore to be scuttled as an artificial reef. (Courtesy of Florida State Archives.)

In 2007, divers explored the wreck of an unidentified sailboat in 315 feet of water off Boca Raton. At the time, there was speculation that the wreck might be the ketch *Charley's Crab*, which disappeared without a trace during a massive storm on March 13, 1993. After cleaning encrustation off the bow, divers found the name of the shipwrecked sailboat to be *Kringeline*. However, just as with *Charley's Crab*, the actual circumstance of this vessel's sinking appears to be a mystery.

Two

RIVER OF GOLD

Mike Mayer is pictured amongst gold and silver bars recovered from the wreck of the *Nuestra Señora de Atocha* following the discovery of a massive cache of treasure in 1985. (Courtesy of Robert Weller.)

This illustration depicts a typical Spanish galleon that sailed from South America and Cuba to Spain. Three major shipwreck events involving the *Nueva España* and *Tierra Firme* fleets occurred off Florida in 1622, 1715, and 1733, with several other minor wrecking events as well. Immediately following the loss of these vessels, a treasure hunt was spawned that continues to this day. (Courtesy of Florida State Archives.)

One of the first modern-day treasure hunters to work the shipwrecks of the 1733 *Nueva España* fleet in the Florida Keys was Art McKee, a commercial diver familiar with the Keys. Here he is suiting up to work on the Seven-Mile Bridge at Moser Channel in 1942. (Courtesy of Art McKee Collection.)

This dramatic image captures Art McKee's salvage of the *capitana*, or flagship, *El Rubi* during the 1950s or 1960s off Tavernier. The *El Rubi* was the flagship of Lt. Gen. Don Rodrigo de Torres and the 1733 fleet. The Spanish salvaged most of the treasure, particularly the gold, after the grounding of the vessel, whereupon the wreck was burned to her waterline. Upon its rediscovery in 1938, McKee used an airlift to help find gold and silver treasure, as well as numerous other 18th-century artifacts. (Courtesy of Art McKee Collection.)

This is another action shot of Art McKee working the wreck of the capitana *El Rubi* during the 1950s or 1960s off Tavernier. The Spanish returned to most of the 1733 shipwreck sites to recover the much-needed treasure. They originally worked several of the 1622 and 1715 wreck sites as well, in some cases using native divers holding their breath and in other situations using a bronze diving helmet. It is interesting to note that salvage efforts on the 1733 wrecks recovered more treasure than originally listed on the ships' manifests, due to the prevalence of contraband gold and silver being carried back by the captain and crew. (Courtesy of Art McKee Collection.)

This gold eight-escudo coin was recovered from a Spanish treasure fleet shipwreck. The escudo, Spanish for "shield," was a unit of currency used from the mid-16th through the early-19th centuries. The gold escudo was issued in different denominations, with the two-escudo coin commonly referred to as a doubloon. (Courtesy of Robert Weller.)

Pictured above, over 100 pieces of oxidized silver are still frozen in the shape of the silk bag that contained them. The coins as well as a K'ang-hsi porcelain cup were recovered off the wreck of the *San Pedro*. (Courtesy of Robert Weller.)

A bronze religious medallion liberated from a coral conglomerate found on a 1733 shipwreck is pictured here. Note the imprint of the medallion in the coral at right. (Courtesy of Robert Weller.)

This olive jar was recovered from the wreck of the *San Pedro*. It is amazing to think this fragile vessel survived a dramatic shipwreck event, as well as almost three centuries underwater, and was found intact. (Courtesy of Robert Weller.)

Pictured above is a coral-encrusted flintlock pistol recovered from one of the 1733 shipwrecks. Most artifacts had to be carefully cleaned of extensive encrustation and then subjected to a lengthy conservation process to stabilize them and prevent deterioration. (Courtesy of Florida State Archives.)

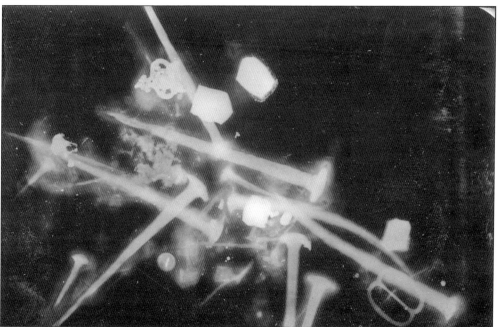

Frequently, numerous artifacts are frozen together in a conglomerate consisting of a mixture of sand, calcareous growth, and ferrous material. In some instances, a diver has no idea that precious artifacts are hidden in a nondescript lump resting amongst the wreck. Only by x-ray analysis is one aware of the secrets hiding inside. Here an X-ray reveals coins, spikes, and a silver crown-shaped medallion nestled in a conglomerate. (Courtesy of Robert Weller.)

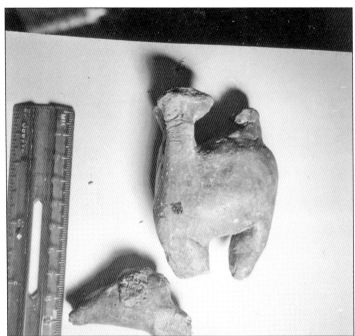

Aside from gold and silver treasure, swords, and cannons, everyday items were also found during the salvage of the 1733 shipwrecks. Here is a figurine recovered from the wreck of the *Herrera*. Due to the abundance of these figurines, the wreck was bestowed the appropriate local moniker of "Figurine Wreck." (Courtesy of Florida State Archives.)

This publicity photograph captures Art McKee at his Museum of Sunken Treasure on Plantation Key. Opened in January 1952, it replaced a smaller museum McKee opened a few years earlier. In this image, he is seen kneeling next to an outdoor recreation of a Spanish shipwreck, complete with ballast pile, timber, and cannons. (Courtesy of Florida State Archives.)

This underwater photograph of *El Gallo Indiano* illustrates what a 1733 wreck site currently looks like. Typically, the only trace of a shipwreck is the large ballast pile carried in the lower portion of the hull for stability. *El Gallo Indiano* served as the *almiranta* of the 1733 fleet; an almiranta, similar to a capitana, was a well-armed galleon that covered the rear of the convoy. (Courtesy of Denis B. Trelewicz Collection.)

Sometimes treasure hunters themselves add to the number of shipwrecks resting on the bottom. This image depicts the final resting spot of the *Rosalie*, one of Art McKee's salvage vessels. The *Rosalie* was a 110-foot long ex-navy subchaser that sank in 1966 or 1967 after catching fire on a return trip from the Caribbean. Her remains still rest in the channel off Plantation Key. (Courtesy of Florida State Archives.)

In this photograph, a solitary cannon points out from a coral outcrop at Elbow Reef off Key Largo. It should be noted that the presence of a cannon does not necessarily suggest an associated wreck, as cannon were occasionally thrown overboard to lighten a grounded vessel. (Courtesy of Denis B. Trelewicz Collection.)

Another treasure salvor who worked the 1733 shipwrecks was Robert "Frogfoot" Weller. In this photograph, he is diving on the *Nuestra Señora de Balvaneda*, better known as *El Infante*, or "the Prince"—Spanish ships typically had several names. The formal name of a ship was based on a patron saint or saints. As these names could be quite long, the ship's name was often truncated or simply associated to the captain or owner, or sometimes a nickname was used to expedite the inclusion of a vessel in a logbook or report to the crown. (Courtesy of Robert Weller.)

Another shot shows Robert Weller on *El Infante* in the late 1960s. Dressed out in standard diving gear of the day, including a double-hose regulator, he inspects a few coins he has found on the wreck site. (Courtesy of Robert Weller.)

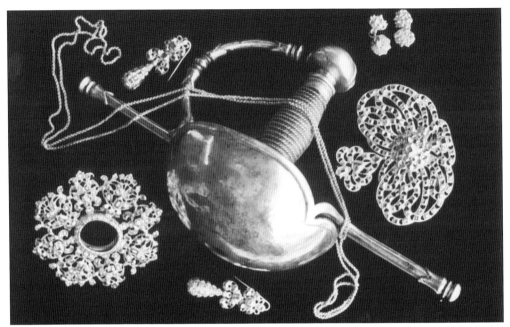

Encompassed in this image is a variety of artifacts recovered off a 1715 fleet shipwreck. Included are several ornate gold brooches, the hilt of a Spanish officer's sword, a gold chain, and gold earrings. While the 1715 wrecks have been worked by modern salvors since the 1950s, spectacular finds are still made each year. (Courtesy of Robert Weller.)

Here are two remarkable artifacts recovered from the 1715 wrecks off the central east coast of Florida. At left is a gold prayer book frame recovered by Andy Matroci on the wreck of the *Nuestra Señora de Las Nieves*. At right is an Immaculate Conception brooch recovered by John Berrier on the wreck of the *Nuestra Señora de Carmen y San Antonio*. (Courtesy of Robert Weller.)

On July 20, 1985, after 16 years of searching, the main pile of treasure from the *Nuestra Señora de Atocha* was found. The site was described by divers as a reef of silver bars. In this underwater image, a stack of silver bars from the *Atocha* rests on the bottom awaiting recovery. In addition to silver and gold bars, copious amounts of emeralds were also found in the area. (Courtesy of Robert Weller.)

Pictured are *Atocha* salvors using a modified shopping cart to haul silver bars up from the water. When the mother lode was located, Mel Fisher was not on site and nowhere to be found. Eventually, as word spread throughout Key West, an all-points-bulletin was issued by the local police department, and requests were broadcast on the local radio station trying to locate Fisher. Ultimately, as Fisher humorously put it, he was literally the last one in the Florida Keys to know about the discovery. (Courtesy of Robert Weller.)

One of the vessels used by Mel Fisher during the salvage of the *Atocha* and *Santa Margarita* was the *Arbutus*. The *Arbutus* was formerly a 175-foot-long U.S. Coast Guard buoy tender built in 1933. She is photographed here in 1979 after she was towed out to the Quicksands to act as a sentry vessel to prevent poachers from working the *Atocha* site. (Courtesy of Florida State Archives.)

The neglected *Arbutus* eventually sank at anchor at the Quicksands. In this image from the early 1980s, the wreck provides a scenic destination for local fishermen. The wreck of the *Arbutus* was also used by Jimmy Buffett for the back cover shot of his greatest hits album, *Songs You Know by Heart*. (Courtesy of George Detrio.)

Over the years, the *Arbutus* slowly settled deeper into the grip of the Quicksands, a sandy shoal area west of the Marquesas Keys. As visible in this photograph from 2005, the only trace of her left visible above water is the mast, which lists to one side. The wreck is still a popular fishing spot, and sightseeing planes headed to Fort Jefferson in the Dry Tortugas commonly fly over the wreck.

Sometimes treasure salvors happened upon other historic shipwrecks in their pursuit of gold and silver. Following Art McKee's introduction to treasure hunting on the capitana *El Rubi*, Charles Brookfield approached him about another potential treasure wreck on Carysfort Reef off Key Largo. On and around a large ballast pile rested 54 cannons. Upon recovery of the iron cannons, however, they found a Tudor rose, indicating English origin. Further investigation determined the wreck to be the HMS *Winchester*, a fourth-rate man-of-war that wrecked on Carysfort Reef on September 24, 1695. In this image, numerous cannons recovered from the *Winchester* line the deck of a work barge in 1938 or 1939. (Courtesy of Art McKee Collection.)

Displayed in this image are the remains of a clock recovered from a coral conglomerate off the wreck of the HMS *Winchester*. Numerous cannons, silverware, small arms, coins, and personal effects were also recovered and featured in a December 1941 *National Geographic* article. Unfortunately, many of the recovered iron cannons from the *Winchester*, as well as the 1733 shipwrecks, were not conserved properly, and over the years, rust has seriously deteriorated those on display along U.S. Highway 1 in the Florida Keys. (Courtesy of Art McKee Collection.)

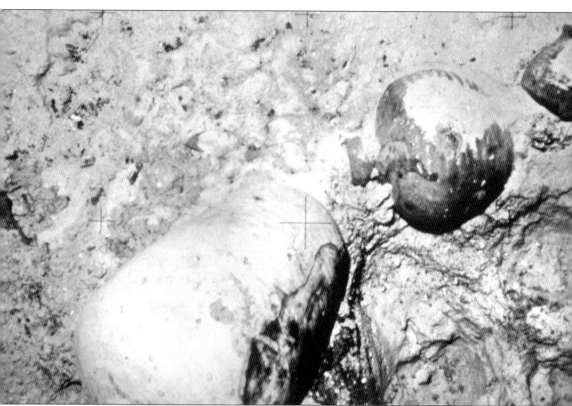

The quest for gold has even led treasure hunters into deep water. In 1965, the trawler *Trade Winds* hauled up some Spanish olive jars and other artifacts from approximately 1,500 feet of water off the Dry Tortugas. In 1989, Seahawk Deep Ocean Technology relocated the wreck. Here their remotely operated vehicle (ROV) is documenting several olive jars and other pottery on the seafloor. Based on analysis of recovered artifacts, it is believed the "Dry Tortugas Shipwreck" is one of three 1622 vessels traveling with the *Atocha* lost in deep water. (Courtesy of Odyssey Marine Exploration.)

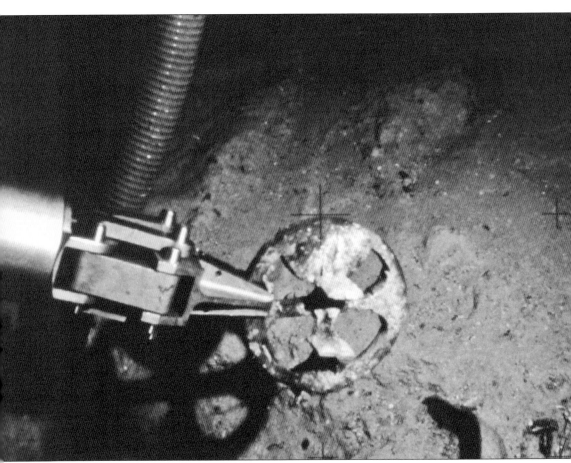

In this 1990 image, Seahawk Deep Ocean Technology's ROV is recovering one of three bronze navigational astrolabes found on the Dry Tortugas Shipwreck. Mariners' astrolabes were used to determine the latitude of the ship at sea by measuring the noon altitude of the sun or the meridian altitude of a star of known declination. (Courtesy of Odyssey Marine Exploration.)

Three

COURSING WATERS

This undated photograph shows an unidentified steamer negotiating the narrow Ocklawaha River in North Central Florida. Unlike wide rivers such as the Mississippi, which hosted massive riverboats, Florida's interior rivers were shallow, winding, and full of submerged hazards, and required a special type of vessel suited for this environment. (Courtesy of Florida State Archives.)

Photographed in 1895, the steamer *Mistletoe* travels across Tampa Bay. The *Mistletoe*, 75 feet long and 16 feet wide, was built at Norwalk, Florida, in 1895. Her standard schedule carried her between Sarasota and Tampa, hauling cargo fuel, pine, mail, and the only supply of ice for Sarasota. She sank in the Hillsborough River during the October 1910 hurricane but was later raised, rebuilt, and renamed the *City of Sarasota*. (Courtesy of Florida State Archives.)

This undated photograph shows the rebuilt *City of Sarasota*, formerly the *Mistletoe*. It was not uncommon for small steamers to be salvaged and put back into service when lost in shallow water. The *City of Sarasota's* career as a passenger and freight steamer ended in November 1919 after again sinking in Tampa Bay. She was raised a second time and converted into a barge, which burned near Snead Island a short time later. (Courtesy of Florida State Archives.)

Fire was a constant threat for mariners, particularly on wooden steamers. Boiler explosions and fires were not uncommon, and numerous steamers were lost in this manner. In this image is the burned hulk of the passenger steamer *Bay Queen* at a Tampa dock in July 1921. The 165-foot long *Bay Queen* was originally built as the *Clermont* at Brooklyn, New York, in 1892. (Courtesy of Florida State Archives.)

The late 1885 photograph above shows the small steamer *Walkatomica*. This vessel was built in landlocked Tallahassee by Capt. William Slusser, and when completed in June 1885, she was put on a Florida Railway and Navigation Company flatcar for the three-hour trip to the coast. She made regular runs to Newport, Carrabelle, and St. Teresa but was ultimately lost to fire on October 4, 1898. (Courtesy of Florida State Archives.)

Photographed on March 13, 1904, the screw steamer *City of Tampa* was lost to fire on June 29, 1921, near Bay Point Light. She was 89 feet in length, 19 feet in breadth, and built in 1887 at Mason City, West Virginia. (Courtesy of Florida State Archives.)

Yet another victim of fire was the steamer *Captain Fritz*, pictured here. Built in 1892 at a Mississippi shipyard, the 100-foot-long steamer was named after its captain and owner, Fritz Bludworth of Defuniak Springs, Florida. On September 19, 1930, the steamer caught fire, burned to the waterline, and sank. One life was lost in the incident. (Courtesy of Florida State Archives.)

The 137-foot-long steamer H. B. *Plant* burned to the water's edge in Lake Beresford, a large lake off the St. Johns River north of Orlando, on the morning of April 29, 1890. The fire, first discovered at 3:45 a.m., was caused by a lamp explosion—a watchman tried to refill the lamp while it was still burning. Cries of "fire" echoed throughout the ship, and passengers in their nightclothes quickly started flocking to the upper rear deck in search of safety. In the end, all but three lives were saved. She is pictured here shortly after her completion at Wilmington, Delaware, in 1880. In 1913, a second steamer named H. B. *Plant* was lost to fire after burning at its pier in Tampa. (Courtesy of Florida State Archives.)

The steamer *Thomas A. Edison*, shown here while resting at dock on the Caloosahatchee River, was a passenger packet steamer built in 1904 at Apalachicola. She was 80 feet long, 21 feet wide, and displaced 33 tons. Constructed with two decks housing 11 staterooms, she was employed on the upriver Caloosahatchee run but was also used twice a week by the Plant ferry service between Punta Gorda and Fort Myers. (Courtesy of Florida State Archives.)

Here is another view of the *Thomas A. Edison* taken in 1910 at Alva, Florida. Thomas Edison and his wife, Mina, would occasionally charter this vessel on excursions to Sanibel Island. On the night of January 30, 1914, the Lee County Packing House caught fire. The *Edison* was tied up at the facility's dock with a full load of fruit when fire, carried by strong winds, ignited the steamer. (Courtesy of Florida State Archives.)

Pictured above, the steamer *Terra Ceia*, built in 1882 at Jacksonville, sank in the Hillsborough River during the October 1910 hurricane that also claimed the steamer *Mistletoe*. However, unlike the *Mistletoe*, the *Terra Ceia* proved to be a total loss. She was 126 feet long, 31 feet wide, and displaced 243 tons. (Courtesy of Florida State Archives.)

The 70-foot-long sternwheeler *Suwannee*, pictured above, was Thomas Edison's favorite steamer for traveling to Florida's east coast. The three-day trip took the steamer from Fort Myers to Fort Lauderdale through the heart of the Everglades. Built at Branford in 1888, the *Suwannee* wrecked during the September 1926 hurricane. However, Henry Ford salvaged portions of the sunken steamer to rebuild it for his friend Thomas Edison. (Courtesy of Florida State Archives.)

sunk in collision
Feb. 16, 1910

This photograph, taken on February 16, 1910, captures the shattered hull and demolished deckhouse of the steamer *Magic City*, which was rammed by the *Parthian* near Mayport on the St. Johns River. Built in 1876, the *Magic City* operated for the Cook Steamship Company at the time of her loss. (Courtesy of Florida State Archives.)

In this 1909 image, the stern-wheel steamer *Calhoun* is partially sunk and resting on the bottom of the Chipola River after hitting a snag. The 46-ton *Calhoun* was built in 1907 at Chipola and was based out of Apalachicola. (Courtesy of Florida State Archives.)

At 3:00 a.m. on March 19, 1903, the Lucas Line steamer *Metamora* sank while running up the Acklawaha River. Because the passengers were all asleep and the steamer sank with little warning, it was a miracle that only two lives were lost. The image above illustrates the interesting inboard stern-wheel configuration of the *Metamora* as she cruises along a narrow river. The *Metamora* was built at Palatka, Florida, and was 87 feet long, 22 feet wide, and displaced 165 tons. (Courtesy of Florida State Archives.)

The *City of Hawkinsville*, pictured here while moored at a dock on the Suwannee River, was a 140-foot-long river steamer built in 1886 by Hawkinsville (Georgia) Deepwater Boat Lines. In 1900, she was sold to Gulf Transportation of Tampa and was used primarily to haul timber on the Suwannee River. With the spread of rail lines through Florida, steamboats became obsolete in the early 1900s. Having outlived its usefulness, the *City of Hawkinsville* was abandoned on the Suwannee River in 1922. (Courtesy of Florida State Archives.)

Since these utilitarian vessels could not be efficiently adapted for other purposes, numerous steamers were left to rot on riverbanks throughout Florida. Fortunately for divers, the *City of Hawkinsville* eventually settled in water deep enough to offer protection from potential salvors or vandals. The *City of Hawkinsville*, which offers a rare glimpse into 19th-century riverine commerce, was designated a Florida Underwater Archaeological Preserve in 1992. Here the steamer is docked at Branford, in close proximity to her final resting spot. (Courtesy of Florida State Archives.)

The steam paddle-wheel steamer *St. Sebastian*, seen here at Rockledge, was launched from the Wilmington, Delaware, shipyard of Pusey and Jones on November 19, 1889. Built for the Jacksonville, Tampa, and Key West Railway, she was 130 feet long, 24 feet wide, and had accommodations for 150 passengers. Capt. Steve Bravo served on the *St. Sebastian* before taking command of the *St. Lucie*, as mentioned in an earlier chapter. (Courtesy of Florida State Archives.)

In this undated photograph, the steamers *St. Sebastian* and *St. Augustine* lay abandoned and deteriorating in the Loxahatchee River. While many steamers were allowed to rot and disappear over several decades, some wrecks were removed as obstructions or hazards. The ultimate fate of these two particular wrecks is unclear. (Courtesy of Florida State Archives.)

The steamer *Mary Disston*, photographed here around 1890 or 1891 while at Tarpon Springs, was built in 1884. She was originally employed to carry mail between Tampa and Bradenton but lost the contract due to missed transfers. Dubbed "Dirty Mary" due to the plumes of black smoke produced by her boilers, she was later sold to the Orange Belt Railroad to support a run between Cedar Keys, Tarpon Springs, and Clearwater. Around 1892, while moored at Gulfport, fire broke out on the *Mary Disston*. She eventually drifted off, burned to her waterline, and sank beneath the surface of Tampa Bay where her remains exist to this day. (Courtesy of Florida State Archives.)

In the shallow waters of Troy Springs reside the skeletal remains of a wreck thought to be the steamer *Madison*, built in 1855. Operated by Capt. James Tucker, the *Madison* was a fixture on the Suwannee River for several years prior to the Civil War. In 1863, Captain Tucker and his troops were ordered to Virginia to serve in the infantry there. Without a crew, he reportedly ordered the ship scuttled at or near Troy Springs, where the ship could not fall into enemy hands. This underwater photograph depicts the current disposition of the alleged wreck of the *Madison*.

Here is a picture of the *Hiawatha* at Silver Springs. The Hiawatha was an inboard stern-wheel steamboat that cruised the Oklawaha River for the Hart Line. She was built at East Palatka in 1898 and was registered with a length of 89 feet, a beam of 27 feet, and a displacement of 129 gross tons. (Courtesy of Florida State Archives.)

Nightfall did not prevent the operation of Florida river steamers. This illustration depicts the *Hiawatha* running up the Ocklawaha River at night. Prior to electricity, a fire was typically set on the top deck to illuminate the surrounding area and facilitate navigation in tight areas of the river. (Courtesy of Florida State Archives.)

Like so many other river steamboats, the *Hiawatha* was left to rot on the banks of the St. Johns River at the end of her career. In 1919, she was grounded at Hart's Point near East Palatka and abandoned. Photographed here in June 1963, the derelict was finally removed in the early 1980s. (Courtesy of Florida State Archives.)

This parting shot, taken in 1954, shows the remains of the steamer *David L. Yulee* near the mouth of the Suwannee River. This steamer was named after Florida senator David Levy Yulee, who was known as the "father of Florida's railroads" because of his tenure as president of four different railroad companies in the late 19th century. (Courtesy of Florida State Archives.)

Four

LEGACY OF WAR

In this somber image, sailors aboard the USS *Biddle* look on as massive plumes of smoke rise from a sea of burning oil that marks the spot where the tanker *Cities Service Empire* was sent to the bottom off Cape Canaveral on February 22, 1942. Following the arrival of German U-boats off Florida, numerous unprepared tankers and freighters were sunk in short order. (Courtesy of Mark Mondano Collection.)

While the majority of the Civil War raged in states farther north, Florida had its share of skirmishes. In this illustration, sailors from the Union frigate *Colorado* launch a sneak attack on Pensacola and the schooner *William H. Judah* in the early hours of September 14, 1861. The raiders successfully torched the *Judah*, which later drifted from her moorings, burned to her waterline, and sank opposite of Fort Barrancas. This raid resulted in the first loss of life in Florida during the Civil War; nearly 20 percent of the raiding party was killed or wounded in the event. (Courtesy of Florida State Archives.)

Above is an illustration depicting the surprise Confederate attack on the side-wheel steamer USS *Columbine* on the St. Johns River. On May 23, 1864, Capt. John J. Dickson and the Confederate 2nd Florida Cavalry ambushed the 132-ton Union tug as it steamed up the river. The Confederates suffered no casualties in the well-executed attack; however, over 148 men onboard the *Columbine* were killed or wounded in the melee, many of whom drowned while attempting to swim across the St. Johns River. The *Columbine* burned to its waterline and sank into the murky St. Johns. (Courtesy of Florida State Archives.)

Capt. John J. Dickson, pictured here, and his small detachment of men were successful in their harassment of Union forces along the river. On March 27, 1863, Captain Dickson ambushed the large transport *Mary Benton* as it unloaded at Teasdale and Reid's Wharf, resulting in numerous Union fatalities, including the commanding officer, Lt. Col. Liberty Billings. Dickson's small force only suffered one minor injury. The 1864 sinking of the *Columbine* represented an uncommon instance in which a warship was destroyed by land-based forces during the Civil War. (Courtesy of Florida State Archives.)

The first American vessel to be lost off Florida due to enemy action occurred in February 1942; however, the first war loss actually occurred over a year earlier. The German freighter *Rhein* was built in Bremen by Aktien-Gesellschaft Weser for the Hamburg-America Line in 1926. The 6,049-ton ship was 454 feet long, 58 feet wide, and powered by an oil-burning engine. Trapped in Mexico at the outbreak of World War II, she eventually fled for Germany in December 1940. U.S. Navy warships shadowed the freighter and reported its position to approaching British and Dutch warships. Cornered off the Dry Tortugas on December 11, the *Rhein*'s crew attempted to scuttle the vessel to prevent its capture. The HMS *Caradoc* finished off the freighter with its deck gun. (Courtesy of Historical Archive of Hapag-Lloyd AG, Hamburg.)

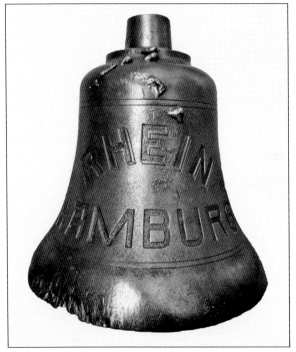

When it was first explored in 1990, divers originally thought the wreck was that of the Panamanian freighter *Hermis*, sunk on June 6, 1942. Billy Deans led a team to recover a bell on the forward deck in 1991, which ultimately led to the identification and story behind the *Rhein*. This auxiliary bell from the crow's nest was recovered in 2001. Note the soldered metal toward the top and the thinned, stretched lip at the bottom—signs of intense heat stress from the fire set by the crew in the attempt to scuttle the ship.

Kapitänleutnant Ulrich Heyse of the *U-128*, pictured here, was the first U-boat commander to arrive off Florida. In just a few days in February 1942, Heyse sent the tankers *Pan Massachusetts* and *Cities Service Empire* to the bottom off Cape Canaveral. Heyse sank a total of almost 84,000 tons of shipping during five war patrols. Even more impressive, he was a German submariner who survived the war. (Courtesy of Mark Mondano Collection.)

Kapitänleutnant Reinhard Hardegen started his naval career in April 1933. Pictured in the control room of the *U-123*, Hardegen conducted five war patrols, resulting in the sinking of almost 116,000 tons of shipping. On January 14, 1942, Reinhard Hardegen made headlines when he sank the Panamanian tanker *Norness* off New York, the first war loss off the coast of the United States. On his last patrol, Hardegen moved down the coast of Georgia and into Florida, leaving a trail of sunken ships. Included in his Florida tally are the tanker *Gulfamerica* off Jacksonville and the freighters *Korsholm* and *Leslie* off Cape Canaveral. Hardegen also survived the war. (Courtesy of Mark Mondano Collection.)

Pictured here are Kapitänleutnant Peter Erich Cremer (center, in the white cap) and the *U-333* upon its return to base at La Pallice, France, on May 26, 1942, following its second war patrol. The middle two pennants signify the sinking of the tanker *Halsey* and the freighter *Amazone* off the Florida coast. Note the damage to the conning tower and periscope as a result of being rammed by the British freighter *Prestige* on the journey to the Florida coast in late April 1942. While Kapitänleutnant Cremer completed nine war patrols, he was only able to amass 36,000 tons of shipping. Perhaps his most notable achievement was that he was one of a minority within the *Unterseebootwaffe* (Germany's submarine force) to survive the war. (Courtesy of Mark Mondano Collection.)

The *Pan Massachusetts*, originally laid down as the *War Cape*, was one of the many merchant vessels built during the waning days of World War I. Wartime hostilities concluded, however, before her completion, and she was ultimately launched as the *Triumph* in January 1919. She is pictured here as the *Triumph* before her conversion and name change to *Pan Massachusetts* in 1938. At 1:44 p.m., on February 19, 1942, two torpedoes fired from *U-128* struck the port side of the 456-foot-long tanker as she was steaming north off Fort Pierce. The resulting explosions and fire broke the ship in two; the stern half sank relatively quickly, while the bow half capsized and floated several miles before sinking in 290 feet of water off Cape Canaveral. While the bow section has been dived, the stern section has yet to be found. The sinking of the *Pan Massachusetts* represented the first of many American war casualties off Florida in World War II. (Courtesy of Mark Mondano Collection.)

The 465-foot long tanker *Cities Service Empire* was built as the *Ampetco* in 1918 at Sparrows Point, Maryland, by the Bethlehem Steel Shipbuilding Company. As the U-boat threat grew in late 1941, the *Empire* was outfitted with a 5-inch deck gun mounted onto a round deck structure on the extreme stern of the tanker, as seen in this image. With Capt. William F. Jerman at the helm, the fully-loaded *Cities Service Empire* approached Cape Canaveral on the morning of February 22, 1942, en route from Port Arthur to Philadelphia, Pennsylvania. At the same time, Kapitänleutnant Ulrich Heyse of *U-128* was sitting quietly on the seabed. Upon hearing the approaching target, *U-128* quickly surfaced and attempted to plot a firing solution. After missing with his first four torpedoes, Heyse slammed two torpedoes into the starboard side of the tanker, instantly igniting a massive blaze that ran the length of the doomed vessel. As the inferno spread, the bow of the crippled tanker slipped under the Atlantic. The stern of the *Cities Service Empire* soon followed, rising clear of the surface and eventually plunging toward the bottom. Fifteen men perished in the attack, including 28-year-old Captain Jerman, who was crushed by a lifeboat as he attempted to save one of his crewmen. (Courtesy of Mark Mondano Collection.)

These rare images capture the events immediately following the sinking of the *Cities Service Empire*. The destroyer USS *Biddle* was the first vessel on the scene and proceeded to pick up oil-soaked survivors. Herbert Goeler was one of the young sailors onboard the *Biddle*, and in a painful interview with this author, he told how they tried in vain to reach the crippled *Empire*. Goeler related how the intense flames kept them at bay, and they were forced to watch helplessly as the tanker began to sink quickly by the bow. Many of the crew members who had sought refuge from the fire on the painter's stage were now forced to jump for their lives. Fortunately, for those who managed to jump clear of the inferno, the Gulf Stream carried them away from the burning sea over the sunken tanker. (Courtesy of Mark Mondano Collection.)

This 2007 underwater image captures the stern deck gun on the wreck of the *Cities Service Empire*. While the defensive guns placed on numerous freighters and tankers definitely looked lethal, they ultimately had little effect in deterring U-boat attacks during World War II. The wreck of the *Empire* rests in approximately 240 feet of water, 30 miles east of Cape Canaveral.

The wreck has been significantly affected by almost seven decades in salt water. The wreck rests close to the western edge of the Gulf Stream, and it is not uncommon for strong currents to wash over the site. The influence of the Gulf Stream has stressed hull members and accelerated the wreck's collapse. This image documents the chaotic mess that is the remains of the bridge and forward superstructure. Four deck levels have been reduced to a flattened debris field in which keen readers may see the disarticulated pieces of the ship's compass and binnacle.

The *Halsey*, built in 1920, was one of the numerous tankers produced by the Alameda, California, shipyard of Bethlehem Shipbuilding Corporation Limited. Launched into service for the Malston Company of Delaware, she was 435 feet in overall length with a 56-foot beam. Typical of many tankers, she had a stern deckhouse, while her bridge superstructure was just forward of amidships. (Courtesy of Mark Mondano Collection.)

U3N
ORPEDOED TANKER(8008W-2723N)600'-12" 0704 6MAY42 970BSN 0-106

On May 6, 1942, the *Halsey* was headed to New York with a full load of fuel oil, gasoline, and naphtha taken on in Corpus Christi, Texas. Just before dawn, a torpedo from *U-333* struck her port side, splitting her open amidships. Miraculously, the tanker's highly volatile cargo did not ignite. The engine of the *Halsey* was quickly brought to a stop while the flammable vapors of her cargo slowly enveloped the stricken vessel. Just after 5:00 a.m., the crew worked to escape the sinking *Halsey* in two lifeboats. Surviving the initial explosion, the survivors now found themselves fighting for consciousness amidst the poisonous naphtha fumes that leaked from the slowly settling vessel. Capt. Peter Erich Cremer placed another torpedo into the side of the *Halsey* later that day, which ignited a raging inferno around the stricken vessel. The tanker soon slipped under the surface as her escaping cargo continued to fuel the fire that burned along the surface of the Atlantic. This aerial photograph documents the tanker in between the two attacks and before her eventual sinking off Fort Pierce. (Courtesy of Mark Mondano Collection.)

The tanker *W. D. Anderson*, official number 221648, was built as the *Tamiahua* in June 1921 by the Moore Shipbuilding Company of Oakland, California. Owned by the Atlantic Refining Company of Philadelphia, Pennsylvania, the single-screw tanker was outfitted with a rarely employed 4,000-horsepower, quadruple-expansion engine manufactured by the Hooven, Owens, and Rentschler Company. This picture documents the *W. D. Anderson* as the *Tamiahua* as she rests on the rocks after grounding south of San Francisco, California, in November 1930. Work to repair the damage caused by the grounding took four months and cost over $600,000. At 500 feet in length and 71.2 feet on the beam, the 10,227-ton vessel would become the largest ship sunk off Florida during World War II. (Courtesy of Mark Mondano Collection.)

This U.S. Coast Guard picture captures the *W. D. Anderson* as she appeared in early 1942. Around 7:00 p.m. on February 22, 1942, Korvettenkapitän Hans-Georg Friedrich (Fritz) Poske, onboard *U-504*, observed the blacked-out *Anderson* steaming northward off Stuart. Less than 24 hours after sinking the *Republic*, Poske launched two torpedoes in quick succession. The massive explosions rocked the submerged *U-504*. In the war journal of *U-504*, Poske wrote, "The ship stood, in a fraction of a second, from forward to astern in flames. After 12 seconds, second (torpedo) hits in the stern; the rear part broke off." Fatally wounded, the *W. D. Anderson* quickly dove for the bottom 550 feet down. (Courtesy of William T. Hultgren.)

The *Republic* was a 392-foot tanker built by the Bethlehem Shipbuilding Corporation in Wilmington, Delaware, in 1920. Her christened name was the *Weweantic*, which was later changed to *Liberty Minquas*. This image captures the *Republic* at sea in December 1941, less than three months before her sinking. Owned by the Petroleum Navigation Company of Houston, the 5,287-ton tanker was on her way to Texas when she was torpedoed by *U-504* at 11:00 p.m. on February 22, 1942, three miles east of Jupiter Inlet. As the crew abandoned ship, the *Republic* developed a sharp list. *U-504* surfaced nearby, observing the survivors pull away from the vessel. (Courtesy of Mark Mondano Collection.)

The stern of the *Republic* came to rest on the bottom, though the bow of the tanker protruded from the water with a 40-degree list to starboard. The day after the sinking, two men from Jupiter Inlet rowed out to the wreck to investigate. Leonard Smith described the scene, recounting in an interview, "She wallowed in the waves, lying on her side. Water hissed through her hatches with a fearsome sound. Clothing and wreckage of all sorts drifted back and forth, and the ship groaned as she moved. We found a small wire-haired terrier that had been left aboard when the crew abandoned ship the night before. He was glad to see us." The bow of the *Republic* remained above water for approximately three months. The wreck was eventually demolished as a hazard to navigation, but divers may still find her remains in approximately 50 feet of water. (Courtesy of Florida State Archives.)

This image documents an unidentified sunken tanker off Florida following a U-boat attack in 1942. During this year, Floridians in coastal communities were quite aware of the ongoing battle just offshore. It was not uncommon to hear massive explosions, see burning hulks drifting offshore, or find oil-soaked debris and bodies washed up on the beach. It was not until the dramatic nighttime sinking of the *Gulfamerica* in April 1942, witnessed by thousands at Jacksonville Beach, that Florida finally instituted state-wide coastal blackouts to prevent ships from being silhouetted by lights on the coast. (Courtesy of Florida State Archives.)

The 424-foot *Laertes*, named after the father of Odysseus in Homer's *Odyssey*, was built at the Taikoo Dockyard and Engine Company in Hong Kong in 1919. Departing New York for Bombay, India, the *Laertes* was burdened with 5,230 tons of war material destined to be used against the Japanese in the Pacific theater. Stowed tightly in her cargo holds and packed in shipping containers that were secured to her deck were 3 airplanes, 17 medium tanks, and 20 trucks, amongst other cargo. *U-109* saw to it that none of the war material on the *Laertes* would ever be used by slamming three torpedoes into the side of the valuable target off Cape Canaveral. Resting nine miles offshore, the cargo of war material can be found throughout the site, including a solitary and remarkably intact M3A General Lee tank minus its turret. (Courtesy of John Bax.)

Not every shipping casualty was a direct result of U-boat attacks. Loaded with a cargo of phosphate rock bound for Norfolk, Virginia, the 345-foot *Benwood* steamed out of Tampa Bay on April 8, 1942. Because of rumors of German U-boats in the Atlantic, she traveled completely blacked out. The 544-foot-long tanker *Robert C. Tuttle*, also blacked out, was steaming south en route to Texas. At 12:45 a.m., the captain of the *Tuttle* observed the dark silhouette of the *Benwood* directly in front of his ship and turned to port to avoid a collision. When the captain of the *Benwood* sighted the tanker a few minutes later, he tragically turned his vessel to port and directly into the path of the larger tanker. As a result, the bow of the *Benwood* smashed into the port side of the *Tuttle*. While the *Tuttle* remained afloat, the *Benwood* quickly flooded and settled to the bottom. The wreck of the *Benwood* was later dynamited as a navigational hazard, and she was used by the military for aerial target practice after World War II. The *Benwood* remains one of the more popular shipwrecks off Key Largo, and countless divers visit the site each year. (Courtesy of Robert Weller.)

In the early morning hours of May 9, 1942, Kapitänleutnant Reinhard Suhren in *U-564* sat off the southeast coast, monitoring the shipping lanes. The silhouette of the Panamanian tanker *Lubrafol* appeared on the southern horizon and grew in size as it approached the patient U-boat commander. The *Lubrafol*, built in 1924 in Newcastle, England, for the Gulf Oil Company, was en route to New York from Aruba, carrying 67,000 barrels of no. 2 heating oil for the War Shipping Administration. At 4:15 a.m., as the *Lubrafol* passed approximately three miles off Pompano Beach and the Hillsboro Lighthouse, the telltale thud and subsequent explosion of a torpedo rocked the 7,138-ton tanker. (Courtesy of © National Maritime Museum, London.)

Two torpedoes hit on the starboard side of the *Lubrafol* in short succession, and the ship was quickly engulfed in flames. The captain ordered the engines stopped at once and turned the helm hard over to bring the ship broadside to the wind. The order to abandon ship was given shortly thereafter, and survivors piled into lifeboats to evacuate the sinking ship and escape the growing sea of fire. The tanker did not sink immediately, and the Gulf Stream slowly carried the vessel northward, as demonstrated in this aerial photograph taken the day of the attack. The tanker eventually plunged for the bottom just north of Cape Canaveral, approximately 150 nautical miles from the initial point of attack. (Courtesy of William T. Hultgren.)

The wreck of the *Lubrafol* rests approximately 40 miles off New Smyrna Beach in 180 feet of water. The stern is resting on her starboard side, while the forward section of the wreck is almost inverted. Here diver Andrew Donn examines one of the tanker's massive screws.

Because of the distance and depth of the wreck, as well as the possible influence of the Gulf Stream over the site, the *Lubrafol* is rarely visited by divers. Thus many artifacts still remain on the wreck. In this photograph, diver Andrew Donn inspects the bronze signal horn adjacent to the crow's nest on the *Lubrafol's* forward mast.

German U-boats were not confined to the Atlantic Ocean alone, as the freighter *Norlindo* would unfortunately learn in becoming the first U-boat victim in the Gulf of Mexico. The *Norlindo* was built in 1920 to ply the waters of the Great Lakes by the Superior, Wisconsin, shipyard of Globe Shipbuilding. Originally christened the *Lake Glaucus*, she was 253 feet in length, 44 feet on the beam, and displaced 2,686 tons. She was photographed dockside as the *Volusia*, her name while employed by the Merchants and Miners Transportation Company from 1925 to 1941. At 10:40 a.m. on May 4, 1942, a single torpedo from *U-507* struck the starboard side of the empty *Norlindo*. The attack was noted in the war diary of *U-507*: "The steamer goes down right away at the stern, and in three minutes stands vertical . . . sinks." *U-507* would go on to sink two other ships, the tankers *Munger T. Ball* and *Joseph M. Cudahy*, the following day. Other U-boats would soon follow *U-507*'s destructive entrance into the Gulf of Mexico. (Courtesy of William T. Hultgren.)

The *Baja California* was built for her original Norwegian owner, A. O. Lindvig, in October 1914 by R. Thompson and Sons, Limited, of Sunderland, England. Pictured here in an undated photograph, the steel-hulled freighter was 265.6 feet in length, 38.5 feet in breadth, and displaced 1,648 gross tons. The *Baja California* was en route to Guatemala from New Orleans via Key West with a general cargo when *U-84* and Kapitänleutnant Horst Uphoff spotted her on July 18, 1942, off Naples. Uphoff approached the freighter in the dark and promptly placed two torpedoes into her hull just before midnight. Within 10 minutes, the *Baja California* had turned on its side and sunk beneath the surface. (Courtesy of William T. Hultgren.)

The *Baja California* came to rest in 115 feet of water. The wreck now lies collapsed on her port side, though there are large intact sections that rise high off the bottom. The small freighter carried an assorted cargo at the time of her loss, including cosmetics, medicine, glassware, and several trucks. One of the inverted truck axles is fairly obvious in this underwater image taken in 2005.

The Kriegsmarine was not the only shipping menace during World War II, as the wreck of the 391-foot tanker *Gulfland* can attest. Vessels traveled while blacked out at night in order to avoid running into prowling U-boats. While the lack of navigational lighting may have mitigated the chance of running afoul of a U-boat, it obviously increased the chance of merchant vessels running into one another. On the night of October 20, 1943, the northbound *Gulfland* collided with the southbound tanker *Gulfbelle*, both of which were owned by Gulf Oil Company of New York. The resulting collision ignited a massive fire that covered both vessels from stem to stern, killing 88 men and eventually sending the *Gulfland* to the bottom. (Courtesy of William T. Hultgren.)

The burning *Gulfland*, built in 1918 by the New York Shipbuilding Corporation at Camden, New Jersey, drifted off, eventually grounding on the remains of the *Republic*, which had been torpedoed and sunk on February 21, 1942. The pyre on the wrecked tanker continued for an amazing 53 days before she was finally sunk by the U.S. Navy. There were only four survivors from the *Gulfland*. After the less intense fire on the *Gulfbelle* subsided, she was salvaged. Towed into Port Everglades to be repaired, she eventually returned to service as the Panamanian-flagged *Poucou*. (Courtesy of National Archives.)

These two 1943 images document the *Gulfland* salvage work conducted by former U.S. Navy diver Capt. Richard Brown (wearing dive gear) from the deck of the partially submerged tanker. In September 1944, Captain Brown successfully refloated the sunken *Gulfland*. However, before he could tow his prize back into port, a storm battered the salvaged tanker, shearing off a portion of the weakened bow, which sank back to the bottom of the Atlantic. Fortunately, the bulk of the tanker remained afloat, and Captain Brown was able to tow it into port to be scrapped. (Both, courtesy of Florida State Archives.)

Torpedoed by *U-109* on the night of April 30, 1942, off Cocoa Beach, the stern of the *La Paz* rests on the bottom in this image taken shortly after the attack. *U-109* did not finish off the freighter, thinking it was beyond saving. Coincidentally, so did the War Shipping Administration, who sold the wreck for $10,000 to William Radford Lovett of the Suwannee Fruit and Steamship Company. Lovett recruited a crew of fishermen and high school boys, five professional salvage divers, and an assortment of improvised equipment and went to work on the wreck. (Courtesy of Florida State Archives.)

It took two and a half months to complete the work, which was delayed by setbacks, including an engine room explosion and the constant fear of marauding U-boats in the area. In this dramatic image, one of Lovett's crew scales the rigging of the sunken *La Paz*. As a bonus, a large portion of the freighter's cargo was undamaged, including $50,000 worth of Johnnie Walker Black Label scotch, assorted machinery, and plumbing fixtures. In return for his tenacity and daring, Lovett was able to sell the salvaged *La Paz* back to the War Shipping Administration for a handsome profit. (Courtesy of Florida State Archives.)

In another successful salvage of a sunken merchant ship, this aerial photograph documents work being conducted on the freighter *Delisle* off Jupiter Inlet in 1942. The 321-foot-long *Delisle*, en route from Baltimore to San Juan, was torpedoed by *U-564* on May 4, 1942, approximately 15 miles off Jupiter Inlet. Aside from two crewmen who died in the attack, the ship was safely abandoned, and the crew rowed for shore. As the ship remained partially afloat, the crew returned to the ship the following day and prepared it to be towed to Miami to be repaired and put back in service. The *Delisle* was lost the following year after striking a mine off Newfoundland. (Courtesy of Mark Mondano Collection.)

The USS *Sturtevant* (DD-240), pictured in 1925, was a 314-foot Clemson-class destroyer built by the New York Shipbuilding Company toward the close of World War I. On April 26, 1942, the old four-stacker departed Key West and steamed up the Northwest Channel to rendezvous with a convoy departing the Mississippi River. Just over two hours out of port, a violent explosion lifted *Sturtevant's* stern from the water. General Quarters was sounded, and the destroyer was put in a hard right turn in order to conduct a counter-attack on the suspected submarine. Just after the *Sturtevant* dropped two depth charge barrages, a second explosion blew a large hole in the main deck and knocked off the no. 3 stack. As the destroyer rapidly began to settle, a third burst ripped her keel apart beneath the aft deckhouse. An investigation determined the destroyer wandered into a recently deployed and unmarked minefield. She now rests in two sections in 60 feet of water. (Courtesy of National Archives.)

The *Sturtevant* would not be the only victim of fratricide as a result of the Allied minefield north of Key West. At least three other vessels were lost in this area during 1942, including the freighter *Gunvor*. The Norwegian tramp steamer *Gunvor* was built in 1935 by the Trondhjems Mek Verksted shipyard of Trondheim. Owned by Bachke and Company, the *Gunvor* was 278 feet in length and 43 feet in breadth. On June 13, 1942, the *Gunvor* departed Mobile, Alabama, for Trinidad with a general cargo. On June 14, Capt. Lars Holm Brynildsen inadvertently strayed into the minefield north of Key West. While the majority of the crew safely abandoned ship in lifeboats, two men were killed in the engine room, and Captain Brynildsen was seriously injured when a mine exploded against the *Gunvor's* hull. Like the *Sturtevant*, the wreck of the *Gunvor* currently rests in 60 feet of water north of Key West. (Courtesy of William T. Hultgren.)

This image depicts the U.S. submarine *R-12* and was most likely taken in the early 1930s. The keel of the USS *R-12* was laid down by the Fore River Shipbuilding Company of Quincy, Massachusetts, on March 28, 1918. In 1943, the 189-foot *R-12* was assigned to Key West to serve as a training submarine. Early on the morning of June 12, the *R-12* proceeded to sea for scheduled sound training operations. While preparing for a planned dive at approximately 12:25 p.m., an alarm suddenly sounded from below because of reported flooding. Although immediate orders were given to blow the main ballast tanks and close the hatches, the ship sank in an estimated 15 seconds. Forty-two sailors, including two Brazilian navy observers, perished as the submarine came to rest in 560 feet of water. It is speculated that the torpedo tube doors malfunctioned, allowing both the outer and inner doors to open at the same time, resulting in a catastrophic flooding event. (Courtesy of National Archives.)

This interesting image, thought to have been taken in the late 1960s, is of a target vessel west of the Marquesas Keys known locally as the "Patricia Target Ship." It illustrates one potential fate for obsolete weapons of war. Over the years, the wreck has been pummeled by navy, air force, and air national guard aircraft and now lies completely submerged. The navy has scuttled several warships off the Florida Keys or used them for various weapons tests. The names or particulars of some ships disappear over time. While the navy and local historians are unsure of the true identity of this vessel, this author believes it to be the fast-attack transport USS *Weber* (APD-75), which was transferred to Key West and used as a target in 1962. (Courtesy of Historical Museum of Southern Florida.)

The German U-boat scourge largely came to an end by 1943 when Allied planners employed escorted convoys and better aerial coverage. What was initially an effective weapon soon became a death trap for thousands of German men, as radar and sonar eliminated the protective cloak of the vast ocean, and U-boats were easily located and sunk. However, German scientists and engineers were busy developing the next generation of submarines, which had greater range, duration, and stealth, and ultimately appeared in the form of the Type XXI U-boat. Development came too late for the Type XXI to be employed in combat. One of these *elektroboats*, *U-2513*, was actually commissioned into the U.S. Navy after the war. After thorough testing, it was sunk during weapons tests in October 1951. This unique warship, the first true modern submarine, now rests in 215 feet of water off the Dry Tortugas. These two underwater images of the conning tower of *U-2513* offer a glimpse of the only German U-boat sunk off Florida. With the exception of *U-157*, which was lost in deep water in the Florida Straits between the Florida Keys and Cuba in 1942, no U-boats were lost off Florida during World War II combat.

Five

THAT SINKING FEELING

This image captures the steamer *Chatham*, sunk at the mouth of the St. Johns River in January 1910, with her bow resting on the bottom. Constructed of iron in September 1884 at a Philadelphia, Pennsylvania, shipyard, the *Chatham* boasted a length of 265 feet, a beam of 40 feet, and a displacement of 2,729 tons. On the morning of January 14, 1910, the Merchants and Miners Company steamer was finishing up her trip from her home port of Baltimore, Maryland, to Jacksonville, Florida, when she soundly struck the north jetty at the entrance of the St. Johns River. The collision resulted in a massive hole in the *Chatham*'s hull, instantly turning the steamer into a complete wreck as water flooded the ship's hold. After being stripped down, the *Chatham* was abandoned, but sections of her iron hull are still popular with local fishermen today. (Courtesy of © The Mariner's Museum, Newport News, Virginia.)

Designed by William Doughty, the USS *Alligator* was the last of five U.S. Navy schooners built specifically to arrest the slave trade and eliminate piracy on the high seas. The keel of the topsail schooner *Alligator* was laid down on June 26, 1820, at the Charlestown Navy Yard in Boston, Massachusetts. However, her noble career was short, because on November 19, 1822, en route to Virginia, the *Alligator* wrecked on the reef that now bears her name. (Courtesy of Florida State Archives.)

This image documents the fate of the four-masted schooner *Clifford N. Carver*, as she rests bilged on Tennessee Reef on April 2, 1913. The 1,100-ton *Carver* was built in 1900 at Bath, Maine, and was 189 feet long and 39 feet wide. (Courtesy of Florida State Archives.)

This engraving, which appeared in the April 1859 issue of *Harper's New Monthly Magazine*, is entitled "Wreckers at Work." Once word of a grounded vessel got around, numerous schooners of the local wrecking fleet would arrive on the scene to see if there was available work. (Courtesy of Florida State Archives.)

WRECKERS AT WORK.

THE DIVERS.

Divers were heavily utilized by the wrecking fleet, but it was a dangerous job. Because of the invading seawater, cargo would inevitably foul and create a hazardous, sometimes toxic, working environment. The mixture of chemicals such as dyes, oil, paints, and drugs, as well as rotting material such as fish and rice, could seriously impair a diver's health. Frequently, divers were temporarily blinded after working in fouled cargo holds. "The Divers," also from the April 1859 issue of *Harper's New Monthly Magazine*, illustrates salvage work within a submerged cargo hold. (Courtesy of Florida State Archives.)

This undated portrait is of Bradish W. Johnson, the "King of the Wreckers." Upon arriving in Key West in 1882, Johnson, known to the locals as "Hog" Johnson, soon became a fixture on the tiny island. For 25 years, he salvaged wrecked vessels along the Florida Keys, first for the Baker Wrecking Company and then for his own Key West Wrecking Company. (Courtesy of Florida State Archives.)

Shown here is the wreck of the steamer *Alicia*, the last great shipwreck for Bradish Johnson and the Keys wrecking fleet. Built at a Glasgow, Scotland, shipyard in October 1883, the *Alicia* was 345 feet in length, 38 feet on the beam, and displaced 2,795 tons. On April 20, 1905, with her cargo holds full of fine silks, linens, silverware, household furniture, machetes, paint, pianos, wine, English ale, and liquor, the *Alicia* slammed onto Ajax Reef and parted her seams. The scattered remains of the steamer can still be found in 20 feet of water in Biscayne National Park. (Courtesy of © The Mariner's Museum, Newport News, Virginia.)

This painting depicts the wooden-hulled screw steamer *America*, built in April 1863. Traveling from Cuba to Boston, Massachusetts, in early 1885, the 166-foot long steamer encountered a winter gale off the Florida coast three days into her trip. Early on the morning of February 11, the captain turned the *America* toward the coast, hoping to beach his vessel after a persistent leak threatened to sink the ship. While rising water extinguished the boiler fires, prevailing winds pushed the steamer toward shore, and she luckily grounded on a sandbar just off the beach. The crew managed to safely abandon ship just moments before the *America* went to pieces off Stuart. (Courtesy of Mark Mondano Collection.)

The scattered remains of numerous wrecks litter the Florida Keys. Thanks to historical accounts and insurance records of salvage efforts, many have been identified, but some are still unknown. One of the most popular unidentified wrecks is "Mike's Wreck," off Key Largo. The skeleton of this vessel rests in shallow water on Elbow Reef. This author believes that "Mike's Wreck" may be the final resting spot of the 165-foot-long steamer *Acorn*, which grounded on Elbow Reef on February 8, 1885.

In addition to divers, fishermen are also attracted to Florida shipwrecks. Over the years, sunken vessels have been transformed into thriving habitat for numerous marine species. Here fishermen test their luck on the submerged hulk of an unidentified military vessel used as a military target off the Marquesas Keys. Following World War II, several former military ships were towed to this area and pummeled by military aircraft. Now none of these are visible above the water's surface. (Courtesy of Florida State Archives.)

In one of the most dangerous occupations in the United States, fishermen are constantly at risk of being lost during their long hours at sea. The hulks of fishing vessels litter the Florida coast. This underwater image captures the broken-down remains of an unidentified trawler off Naples. Typically, the engine, scattered rigging, and running gear of trawlers are all that can be found after any period of time underwater.

Collisions are a constant threat to vessels at sea, even when operating far from busy ports and harbors, as evidenced by the sinking of the *Araby Maid*, pictured here under full sail. The *Araby Maid* was built in October 1868 by Robert Steele and Company of Greenock. An elegant iron-hulled bark, she was 197 feet in length, 32 feet on the beam, and displaced 863 tons. The *Araby Maid* was lost following a collision with the Mallory Line steamship *Denver* on the night of November 21, 1903, approximately 30 miles northwest of the Dry Tortugas. The captain of the *Araby Maid* saw the *Denver* bearing down on his vessel but realized it was too late to save his ship from the imminent collision. Following the impact, the *Denver* backed away, allowing the Gulf of Mexico to flood into the stricken *Araby Maid*. Five minutes after the fateful encounter, the once-graceful sailing ship slipped beneath the surface. Two men, one of whom was the *Araby Maid's* first mate, perished in the accident.

These two underwater images document the wreck of the *Araby Maid*. An elegant sailing vessel when built, the wreck of the *Araby Maid* is just as beautiful. She rests upright and largely intact in 220 feet of clear water at the entrance to the Gulf of Mexico. While the vessel was iron hulled, her decking and superstructure were wood. Over the years, these portions have been consumed by wood-eating teredo worms, leaving a metal-framed skeleton. In the above image, looking forward toward the bow, the V-shaped gash to the port bow resulting from the collision is obvious. In the image below, looking aft toward amidships, the iron deck framing and outline of a cargo hold are visible.

As with many shipwrecks, recreational divers were responsible for the identification of the *Araby Maid*. Billy Deans and Don DeMaria were the first divers to visit the wreck in 1989. At the time, they did not know the identity of the vessel or its history, but simply referred to it as the "Schooner." The following year, Gary Gentile recovered the brass capstan cover, seen here, which identified her as the *Araby Maid*.

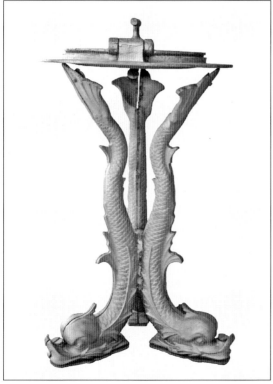

Several other interesting artifacts have been recovered from the *Araby Maid*. Pictured here is the bronze binnacle from the former sailing vessel. A binnacle is a stand that supports the compass used for vessel navigation. The three supporting legs of this unique object were cast to resemble sea serpents, complete with fins and scales.

Vessels designed to improve navigation are just as vulnerable to accidents as any other ship. This image details the 200-foot-long U.S. Army Corps of Engineers hydraulic dredge *Cumberland*, built in 1902 at Belfast, Maine. The *Cumberland* was outfitted with two 18-inch centrifugal pumps to extract sediment from harbor and channels to facilitate safe navigation. On June 23, 1931, the *Cumberland* was en route from Savannah, Georgia, to Mobile, Alabama, when she strayed too close to shore and wrecked just off Fort Lauderdale, reportedly on a pile of cement jettisoned by another vessel that ran aground in the same area in 1913. (Courtesy of U.S. Army Corps of Engineers.)

Another former U.S. Army Corps of Engineers hopper dredge lost off Florida was the *Hydro Atlantic*, originally built as the *Delaware* in 1905. She is pictured in 1938, early in her career. After eight decades removing thousands of tons of material, the *Hydro Atlantic* was destined for a scrap yard in Texas when she sank in approximately 175 feet of water one mile east of the Boca Raton Inlet on December 7, 1987. (Courtesy of U.S. Army Corps of Engineers.)

Reportedly, the operation towing the *Hydro Atlantic* to the scrap yard neglected to maintain the four pumps that were needed to keep the leaky 82-year-old vessel afloat, and she began to wallow behind the tug. By the time the situation was recognized, it was too late. The tug parted the tow lines, and the dredger quickly settled beneath the surface. As seen here in a 2007 underwater image, the *Hydro Atlantic* is a massive wreck. She is largely intact and rises over 50 feet off the sea floor. After 30 years underwater, the rusting dredge ship has been transformed into a kaleidoscope of color by hard and soft corals, and dense schools of tropical fish.

Pictured here in 1916 on the Potomac River is the steam yacht *Isis*. Built in 1902, she served as a patrol vessel during World War I before being used as a survey vessel by the Coast and Geodetic Survey. On January 20, 1920, the *Isis* was taking soundings near a submerged wreck near St. Augustine in preparation for placement of a warning buoy in the area when she accidentally strayed too close and breached her hull. The captain drove the sinking *Isis* up on the beach to allow his crew to safely abandon ship. Before the 180-foot-long yacht could be salvaged, a storm destroyed the *Isis*. She was abandoned in the surf, where she rests to this day. (Courtesy of National Oceanic and Atmospheric Administration.)

As a predecessor to the U.S. Coast Guard, the U.S. Lifesaving Service was formed in 1871 to rescue and aid mariners in distress. In 1875, stations were added along the coast of Florida. Crews manned these stations and patrolled the coast to help in the event of a grounded or wrecked vessel. In this 1890s image, a U.S. Lifesaving Service boat crew from the Jupiter Lifesaving Station aids a family. (Courtesy of Florida State Archives.)

In January 1907, the 209-foot-long Norwegian ship *Ruby* was stranded on a shoal off Fernandina. As a result of damage sustained during the grounding and subsequent salvage, the vessel was condemned. In this picture, the vessel is listing hard to port, with the salvage tug *Wade Hampton* in the background at left. The third vessel is unidentified.

Built in Boston, Massachusetts, by the Atlantic Iron Works, the U.S. Revenue Cutter *Samuel Dexter* was launched in late 1874. She is shown here early in her career. After serving her role in the Revenue Cutter Service, the *Samuel Dexter* was sold on July 18, 1908, to the Aiken Towing Company of Pensacola and renamed the *Leroy*. For almost 20 years, the *Leroy* worked as a tug along the Panhandle before springing a leak and sinking on November 16, 1926, off Panama City. (Courtesy of U.S. Coast Guard.)

Built in 1904 at Philadelphia, Pennsylvania, the Clyde Line freighter *Mohican* was 238 feet long, 40 feet wide, and displaced 2,255 tons. On May 10, 1925, the crew discovered a fire in the aft hold while en route from Jacksonville to Miami with a general cargo. The ship dropped anchor in Canaveral Bight to allow the entire crew to battle the blaze. By the next morning, all that was visible from the beach was the funnel and masts of the smoldering freighter. Her charred hulk was eventually demolished with explosives by the U.S. Coast Guard. (Courtesy of Mark Mondano Collection.)

In this dramatic photograph, the 109-foot-long houseboat *Osiris* is seen burning off Miami on February 12, 1921, while the crew stands by in a launch after abandoning ship. The 137-ton yacht was built in 1911.

Originally built in 1892 in Nelsingfor, Denmark, the *Prins Valdemar* was named for a Danish prince who became a beloved figure to his country by refusing the throne to Bulgaria in 1885. In her stubborn attempts to thwart the salvage efforts following her capsizing in Miami Harbor, the bark *Prins Valdemar* shared more than just a name with the Danish prince. On January 9, 1926, the 226-foot vessel ran aground on the edge of a sandbar in the Miami Shipping Channel. On the following day, the receding tide combined with strong winds destroyed the bark's balance, and the *Prins Valdemar* suddenly careened over on her starboard side, ultimately coming to rest half aground and half submerged across the shipping channel. These two images capture the scene in the wake of the capsizing. (Both, courtesy of Florida State Archives.)

The task of refloating the vessel took 42 days, during which time over 50 vessels carrying millions of dollars of needed building supplies were unable to enter the port to offload their cargo. The delay caused by the sinking of the *Prins Valdemar* resulted in the end of the Miami building boom. After its salvage, the steel bark was hauled ashore to a spot at Bayfront Park, berthed in a bed of concrete, and over the years was employed as an aquarium, restaurant, and a civic center. This image, taken in 1940, documents the *Prins Valdemar* being used as an aquarium. Over time, the landlocked ship started to show her age. In 1952, the city of Miami finally had the *Prins Valdemar* demolished and hauled away. (Courtesy of Alice L. Luckhardt.)

Captured in this image is the *Queen of Nassau* rusting away in Biscayne Bay in 1925. One of the more significant Florida shipwrecks, the *Queen of Nassau* was built as the CGS *Canada* in 1904. Initially serving as the flagship for the Canadian Fisheries Protection Service, she later formed the nucleus of the Royal Canadian Navy. In 1924, she was sold to Barron Collier, one of the largest landowners in the state of Florida. Renamed the *Queen of Nassau*, she was outfitted to carry passengers between Miami and the Bahamas. When that plan failed, she sat idle in Biscayne Bay for two years. In 1926, she departed Miami for a potential sale in Tampa when she sank suspiciously off Islamorada. (Courtesy of © The Mariner's Museum, Newport News, Virginia.)

In this image is the *Northern Light*, a steam freighter built in 1888 by Globe Iron Works of Cleveland, Ohio, for service on the Great Lakes. She was eventually converted into a barge and used along the Atlantic coast. On November 8, 1930, the 300-foot-long barge was in tow behind the tug *Ontario* with a cargo of 3,680 tons of phosphate rock when she was struck by a strong gale off the Florida Keys. The towing cable between the two ships parted, and the *Northern Light*, with an attending crew of six, quickly sank. Only one of her crew, J. Stewart, was rescued by the *Ontario*. (Courtesy of Al Hart.)

Pictured here is the capstan cover from the wreck of the *Northern Light*, which rests in 190 feet of water off Key Largo. Recovery of this artifact led to the identification of the then-unknown wreck, known locally as the "Elbow Wreck." (Courtesy of Ric Altman.)

Resting dockside at Miami in this 1925 image, the freighter *Elizabeth* would meet her fate off the coast of this same city. In November 1935, the *Elizabeth* was driven aground 300 yards off Miami Beach during a hurricane. The *Elizabeth* remained here for over six months before being pulled off and scuttled in 600 feet of water in May 1936. (Courtesy of Florida State Archives.)

Seen here is the schooner barge *Vitric* being towed up the East River in the 1930s. On March 29, 1944, while en route from Havana, Cuba, to West Palm Beach, the 166-foot-long *Vitric* capsized and sank in 310 feet of water off Key Largo. At the time of her loss, the *Vitric* was carrying a cargo of 134,000 gallons of molasses syrup contained in a dozen large tanks on the deck. (Courtesy of Steve Lang.)

Numerous derelicts can be found throughout Florida's waterways. In this image, the collapsed hulk of an unidentified shipwreck rusts in Tampa Bay in the shadow of the Sunshine Skyway.

Known locally as the "Fleming Key Wreck," this abandoned vessel rests in shallow water near Key West. Even with examination by archaeologists, the identity of this vessel is still unknown.

At right is a portrait of John Ringling, who was one of seven brothers who created a traveling circus empire when he merged his own Ringling Brothers Circus with Barnum and Bailey Circus in 1919. John Ringling moved his headquarters to Sarasota in 1927, and numerous dignitaries and politicians were entertained on his personal yacht, *Zalophus*. (Courtesy of Florida State Archives.)

This is John Ringling's yacht *Zalophus*, as featured in an advertisement shortly after its construction in 1922. In March 1926, the 125-foot-long yacht ran aground in Sarasota Bay, stranding New York mayor James J. Walker and three New York newspaper correspondents. Fortunately, damage to the vessel was minor. However, approximately four years later, the *Zalophus* struck a submerged obstruction and sank off Lido Key near Sarasota in the early morning hours of February 4, 1930. Early reports stated a family close to the Ringlings was aboard the yacht. Later information revealed Mayor Walker was again on the yacht, this time with his mistress, actress Betty Compton.

On September 26, 1909, en route from Rotterdam to Jacksonville, the Dutch steamer *Zeeburg* ran aground on the south jetty at the mouth of the St. Johns River. Here she is depicted resting heavily and with her back broken shortly after the event. The 3,039-ton *Zeeburg* was 325 feet long, 49 feet wide, and was launched on August 2, 1899. (Courtesy of Florida State Archives.)

This is an image of the *Vamar* from the late 1930s. While originally christened as the HMS *Kilmarnock* in 1919, this small steamer most notably sailed as the *Eleanor Bolling* in support of Adm. Richard E. Byrd's historic Antarctica expedition. Renamed the *Vamar* in 1933, she sank mysteriously at the mouth of St. Joseph Bay on March 21, 1942. Today the wreck lies scattered on a sandy bottom in 25 feet of water just east of Panama City. (Courtesy of © The Mariner's Museum, Newport News, Virginia.)

In this classic shipwreck image, the yacht *Mandalay* is resting hard aground on Long Reef south of Miami on New Year's Day 1966. Originally built as the *Hardi Biaou* in 1928, the *Mandalay* was 112 feet in length and 24 feet in breadth. At 3:00 a.m. on January 1, 1966, the *Mandalay* grounded on the shallow reef, throwing passengers from their berths. Fortunately, all passengers and crew were safely rescued. The *Mandalay* was slowly picked apart by salvors and heavy seas alike. (Courtesy of Historical Museum of Southern Florida.)

Photographed on January 13, 1941, this dramatic photograph captures the liner *Manhattan* stranded off Palm Beach. Unlike the yacht *Mandalay*, after 22 days aground, the 705-foot-long passenger liner was successfully refloated. This effort required the offloading of tons of cargo, including many automobiles and fuel oil, the dredging of an escape channel, and three salvage tugs before the *Manhattan* was released from its sandy grip on February 4, 1941. (Courtesy of Florida State Archives.)

Some time on the morning of February 4, 1963, the Type T2-SE-A1 tanker SS *Marine Sulphur Queen* disappeared off the west coast of Florida, becoming one of the greatest Florida shipwreck mysteries. The only evidence of her existence was the scant remnants of debris recovered 12 miles southwest of Key West on February 20. No trace of her 39 crewmen was ever found. Pictured here shortly before her disappearance, the *Marine Sulphur Queen* was originally built in 1944 as the *Esso New Haven* by the Sun Shipbuilding Company of Chester, Pennsylvania. At the close of World War II, the ubiquitous Type T2 tankers were rapidly produced by numerous shipyards on both coasts of the United States. Average production time from the laying of the keel to completion for sea trials was an astounding 70 days. In 1961, the *Marine Sulphur Queen* was modified to become the first vessel of its kind to transport molten sulfur. (Courtesy of U.S. Coast Guard.)

The disappearance of the *Marine Sulphur Queen* made headlines throughout the spring of 1963. Theories of her loss ranged from the probable to the absurd. It is possible that the heavily laden ship broke in half in the heavy seas that it encountered; numerous other Type T2 tankers have broken in half in rough weather. These two images document some of the debris recovered from the wreck of the 524-foot-long *Marine Sulphur Queen* during search efforts. Above, a portion of the tanker's name board is inspected, while below, a life ring and preserver are displayed. (Both, courtesy of U.S. Coast Guard.)

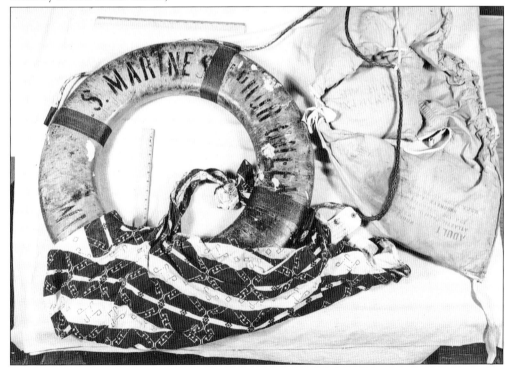

The *Gwalia* was a robust 415-ton, ocean-going tug built in 1907 at a Philadelphia, Pennsylvania, shipyard. A stout vessel, she registered a length of 130 feet and a breadth of 27.5 feet. With Capt. M. D. Cogswell at the helm, the *Gwalia* and a crew of 14 departed Mobile, Alabama, on December 2, 1925, bound for Tampa. In tow was the barge *Altamaha*, burdened with a load of gravel for the Tampa Coal Company. On Friday, December 4, the two vessels encountered a strong winter storm churning in the Gulf of Mexico. Pounded by heavy seas, the *Gwalia* began taking on water from a leak underneath her boilers. The crew hastily left the doomed tug in a single lifeboat, eventually boarding the barge to await rescue several days later, while the *Gwalia* rolled over and slipped beneath the tumultuous surface approximately 85 miles northwest of the mouth of Tampa Bay. Known for decades as the "Middle Grounds Wreck," the tug *Gwalia* was identified in 2004. (Courtesy of © The Mariner's Museum, Newport News, Virginia.)

The 98-foot tug *Point Chicot*, shown here in an undated photograph, was built in Wilmington, Delaware, in 1925. On April 19, 1973, the *Point Chicot* was towing two barges loaded with fertilizer when it sank just before dawn 120 miles west of Tampa Bay. Before they were able to broadcast a Mayday, the crew of the *Point Chicot* were forced to abandon ship. However, they managed to make it to one of the barges and were rescued when a U.S. Coast Guard plane searching for another missing vessel spotted the drifting barges. (Courtesy of Dan Owen.)

A more recent addition to the bottom of the Gulf of Mexico is the tug *Capt. Gil*, which was lost off Steinhatchee on February 6, 1996. The 46-foot-long *Capt. Gil* was built at Houma, Louisiana, in 1952 and was headed to Tampa when the crew noticed water in the engine room. Unlike the *Point Chicot*, the *Capt. Gil* was able to issue an S.O.S. With a U.S. Coast Guard helicopter and a charter boat on scene, the crew jumped ship as the tug sank stern first in 80 feet of water. (Courtesy of Dan Owen.)

Just about every type of ship has been lost off Florida, but maritime casualties are not just limited to surface vessels. One such example is the loss of U.S. Coast Guard Albatross No. 1240, pictured here soon after delivery in 1951, which departed St. Petersburg on March 5, 1967, to assist a sinking vessel off Carrabelle. After passing low to drop a dewatering pump to the 40-foot yacht *Flying Fish*, the aircraft crashed a short distance away. It was not until 2006 that the wreck of the Albatross was identified, and the tragic sacrifice of the six-man crew illustrated how quickly rescuers can become in need of rescuing on the ocean. (Courtesy of U.S. Coast Guard.)

Commissioned into the U.S. Coast Guard on July 20, 1944, the *Blackthorn* was one of 19 Iris-class buoy tenders, which were 180 feet long, 37 feet in breadth, and displaced 984 tons. She is pictured at sea conducting maintenance of navigational aids. At 8:21 p.m. on January 28, 1980, the *Blackthorn* and the 605-foot tanker *Capricorn* collided nearly head-on in Tampa Bay. Because of extensive damage, the *Blackthorn* capsized and sank to the bottom. Twenty-three *Blackthorn* crew members lost their lives in this tragic incident. (Courtesy of U.S. Coast Guard.)

The following images document the salvage of and damage sustained by the buoy tender *Blackthorn* in late January 1980. After the accident, the *Blackthorn* was raised and taken to Tampa, where a formal investigation into the accident was launched. The photograph below demonstrates the massive damage sustained by the buoy tender from the anchor of the *Capricorn*, which lodged in the hull of the *Blackthorn*. Following the investigation, the vessel was stripped, towed offshore of Clearwater, and sunk as an artificial reef. (Both, courtesy of U.S. Coast Guard.)

With advances in modern technology, man has successfully thwarted many of Mother Nature's attempts to sink seagoing vessels. Improved weather forecasting, real-time satellite imagery, and radar allow mariners to avoid most threatening storms. Every so often, though, Mother Nature spawns a tempest and ambushes unsuspecting vessels unfortunate enough to cross her merciless path. In October 1992, one such storm raced through the Gulf of Mexico and pounced on the 255-foot-long freighter *Holsten*. Besieged by 30-foot seas, the freighter foundered approximately 100 miles off Tampa. The *Holsten* is pictured here hauling a typical mixed cargo as the *Terra Nova* in the 1980s.

These two underwater images document the wreck of the freighter *Holsten*. Resting on her starboard side in 200 feet of water, the vessel is completely intact. Divers exploring her forward cargo holds can still find some of the many bags of corn flour. The *Holsten*'s cargo helped to lead a rescue vessel to the scene because the corn flour stained the surface of the Gulf of Mexico along a trail originating at the wreck site. For years until its eventual identification as the *Holsten*, the site was known by fishermen as the "Flour Wreck."

Aside from the thousands of naturally occurring shipwrecks off Florida, hundreds of obsolete vessels have been used as artificial reefs. Recently, military vessels have joined the numerous freighters, tugboats, and barges sunk to serve as marine habitats. One of the most popular is the 510-foot-long USS *Spiegel Grove*, scuttled off Key Largo in 2002. Pictured in 1979, the *Spiegel Grove* could support amphibious invasions by deploying landing ships and hovercraft. (Courtesy of Naval Historical Center.)

The versatile USS *Spiegel Grove* could launch 300 troops in 21 landing craft, as well as from numerous helicopters that could land on the deck above the boat well on the stern. She was also armed with numerous defensive 50-mm and 20-mm anti-aircraft guns, one of which is pictured here on the wreck of the amphibious assault ship.

In May 1944, workers in the New York Navy Yard laid the keel of the last Ticonderoga-class attack aircraft carrier, the USS *Oriskany*. Following 25 years of gallant service, including tours off Korea and Vietnam, the approximately 900-foot-long aircraft carrier was decommissioned in September 1975, stricken from the Naval Vessel Register in July 1989, and eventually scuttled off Pensacola as the world's largest intentionally created artificial reef in May 2006. She is pictured here in her final moments afloat (Courtesy of U.S. Navy.)

This final parting shot captures the island of the aircraft carrier USS *Oriskany* less than 24 hours after its sinking on May 17, 2006. While sunk in 220 feet of water, the massive vessel rises more than 150 feet off the seafloor. Since its deployment as an artificial reef, thousands of divers have explored its submerged remains.

DISCOVER THOUSANDS OF LOCAL HISTORY BOOKS
FEATURING MILLIONS OF VINTAGE IMAGES

Arcadia Publishing, the leading local history publisher in the United States, is committed to making history accessible and meaningful through publishing books that celebrate and preserve the heritage of America's people and places.

Find more books like this at
www.arcadiapublishing.com

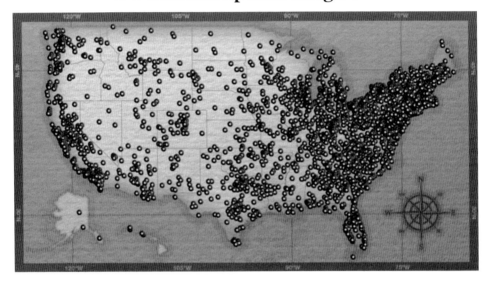

Search for your hometown history, your old stomping grounds, and even your favorite sports team.

Consistent with our mission to preserve history on a local level, this book was printed in South Carolina on American-made paper and manufactured entirely in the United States. Products carrying the accredited Forest Stewardship Council (FSC) label are printed on 100 percent FSC-certified paper.

MADE IN THE USA